WILLIAM WORDSWORTH

Ronald Sands

'Every man has a lurking wish to appear considerable in his native place' wrote Dr Johnson in 1771, and certainly William Wordsworth, born the previous year on 7 April 1770 in the small Cumberland town of Cockermouth, achieved distinction in his native Lake District. He also, through his life and work there, made the region famous the world over. The house where he was born presents a solid, reassuring 18th-century front to the world, but the garden at the back with the River Derwent flowing past, was for the boy William a place of magic and adventure. From an early age he revelled in the beauty and power of natural things:

> Oh! many a time have I, a five years' Child,
> A naked Boy, in one delightful Rill,
> A little Mill-race sever'd from his stream,
> Made one long bathing of a summer's day,
> Bask'd in the sun, and plunged, and bask'd again . . .

His childhood was spent largely in Cockermouth and Penrith where in 1778 his mother died. He seems to have had few memories of her. She thought his temper 'stiff, moody and violent' and confided to a friend that he would be 'remarkable either for good or evil'. He later recalled how he tried to divert Richard, his elder brother, from their game of whip and tops by challenging him to slash a family portrait hanging in his grandparents' drawing room. Richard refused but William struck out at the painting 'for which no doubt, though I have forgotten it, I was properly punished. But possibly, from some want of judgement in punishments inflicted, I had become perverse and obstinate in defying chastisement and rather proud of it . . .'.

Following the death of his mother, William and his brothers spent much of their time in their uncle's house at Penrith, whilst his sister Dorothy was sent to Halifax to stay with relatives. The separation from his sister lasted nine years.

From 1779 until 1787 William attended the grammar school at Hawkshead, lodging with Ann Tyson at Colthouse. The school was founded by Edwin Sandys (later Archbishop of York) in 1585 and the present building, dating from 1675, is open to the public. Under 'Hawkshead's happy roof' William thrived and when the school celebrated its two-hundredth anniversary in 1785 the scholars were encouraged to write verses to honour the occasion. Wordsworth was later very modest about his early attempts to write poetry, but he recognized that this exercise 'put it into my head to compose verses from the impulse of my own mind'. The anniversary composition was certainly impressive for a boy of his age but it reflected—as he later acknowledged—the diction and style of the time, characterized by high-flown terms, personifications and strongly rhymed heroic couplets:

★

LEFT: *The drawing room of Wordsworth's birthplace, a fine house built in 1745 by a sheriff of Cumberland.*

FACING PAGE, ABOVE: *The River Derwent, whose 'ceaseless music . . . composed my thoughts/To more than infant softness . . .'*

FACING PAGE, BELOW LEFT: *The house in Cockermouth where William, his sister and three brothers were all born between 1768-1774. His father, a trained lawyer, was Sir James Lowther's agent.*

FACING PAGE, BELOW RIGHT: *William's 'exquisite sister' Dorothy (1771-1855). Her journals reveal a compassionate, emotional woman completely devoted to her brother.*

And has the Sun his flaming chariot driven
Two hundred times around the ring of heaven,
Since Science first with all her sacred train,
Beneath yon roof began her heavenly reign?
While I thus mused, me thought, before mine eyes,
The Power of Education seemed to rise;
Close at her side were all the powers, designed
To curb, exalt, reform the tender mind:

His time at Hawkshead with his brother Richard
was a happy one and he remained grateful all his life
for the influence of his young headmaster, William
Taylor, who urged him to read and write poetry. He
was thankful also to a master (Mr Shaw) 'who taught
me more of Latin in a fortnight than I had learnt during
two preceding years at the School of Cockermouth'.
He especially enjoyed the freedom he was given, both
at school and during the vacations, to read whatever
he wished. Shakespeare, Milton and Spenser were
among his favourites and he completed the formidable
task of reading all of Fielding's novels as well as relishing
that eternal favourite of young readers, Swift's *Gulliver's
Travels*.

His liking for literature began early. At the age of
nine he treasured 'a yellow canvas-cover'd Book,/A
slender abstract of the Arabian Tales' and when he
learned that there were four large volumes of these
stories he made a pact with another boy jointly to save
up with the intention of purchasing the complete
collection. They remained true to their undertaking
for several months, steadfastly resisting all temptation
to spend, until ultimately their resolve failed and their
project was abandoned.

In addition to this mental freedom to read widely,
he enjoyed considerable physical freedom to roam the
surrounding countryside, to visit Furness Abbey, to
go ice skating, riding, flying kites, fishing and to take
long walks. He also found time to carve his name on
his desk—a signature still visible today. His schoolboy
forays into the countryside came to have a special

significance for him as he felt increasingly the power
and influence exerted over him by the world of nature:

Fair seed-time had my soul, and I grew up
Foster'd alike by beauty and by fear;
Much favour'd in my birthplace, and no less
In that beloved Vale to which, erelong,
I was transplanted.

He guiltily recalled how under cover of the night he
stole captive birds from the traps set by others and
how, riddled with guilt, he felt he was being followed,
hearing:

. . . among the solitary hills
Low breathings coming after me, and sounds
Of undistinguishable motion, steps
Almost as silent as the turf they trod.

These feelings of both 'beauty' and 'fear' in the face
of nature were not uniquely Wordsworthian. In 1772
the picturesque traveller and guide-book writer,
William Gilpin, made famous a quotation of a visitor
who, impressed by Lakeland's scenery exclaimed
'Here is beauty indeed – Beauty lying in the lap of
Horrour!'; but Wordsworth felt these emotions with
an intensity not hitherto expressed. To some extent he
was a child of his time, but he was also a revolutionary
in that his writings ultimately changed the way in

★

ABOVE LEFT: *The Hawkshead cottage often identified as William's
school-time lodgings, although he also lived at Colthouse. Ann Tyson
provided board for his brothers, too.*

ABOVE RIGHT: *Hawkshead Grammar School where William and his
contemporaries were expected to be at their desks by at least six
o'clock in the morning.*

FACING PAGE, ABOVE: *Friar's Crag, Derwent Water. This viewpoint
is recommended by Wordsworth in his 'Guide to the Lakes'.*

FACING PAGE, BELOW: *William's boyhood outings included visits to
Furness Abbey and the Italian marbles in Ings Church.*

which most of us now perceive the natural world.

Winter evenings were often spent with his brothers and friends by Ann Tyson's bright peat fire, playing such games as whist and noughts-and-crosses. They no doubt squabbled from time to time for he admitted 'we were a noisy crew'. These evenings indoors with the sound of winter gales and cracking ice outside must have made their outdoor pastimes the more welcome and enjoyable, especially the skating which he described so vividly:

> All shod with steel,
> We hissed along the polished ice in games
> Confederate, imitative of the chase. . .

Spurred on by the success of his verses on the school's anniversary William began a poem describing the scenery in which he grew up, and his adventures there. Only the conclusion of this poem survives, but it shows his increasing facility in writing verse and reflects, too, his deep attachment to the Lake District countryside:

> Dear native regions, I foretell,
> From what I feel at this farewell,
> That, wheresoe'er my steps may tend,
> And whensoe'er my course shall end,
> If in that hour a single tie
> Survive of local sympathy,
> My soul will cast the backward view,
> The longing look alone on you.
>
> Thus, while the Sun sinks down to rest
> Far in the regions of the west,
> Though to the vale no parting beam

> Be given, not one memorial gleam,
> A lingering light he fondly throws
> On the dear hills where first he rose. ·

This poem was completed in 1787 and that same summer he left Hawkshead School to spend his holidays at Penrith prior to studying at Cambridge University. By now Richard Wordsworth was working in a London solicitor's office. His Penrith vacation with his younger brothers, John and Christopher, was made especially congenial by his reunion with his beloved sister Dorothy. They resumed their excursions together which they had found so pleasurable during their childhood at Cockermouth. For William there was an additional female companion, Mary Hutchinson, an orphan girl living with an aunt in Penrith. Years later Mary became his loyal and devoted wife.

William and Dorothy's joy at being united was, however, short lived: the sour 'Uncle Kit' insisted that he return to Hawkshead before the university term began.

In October 1787 he left for the first time in his life his 'native regions' and he must have been struck by the contrast of the flat countryside as he entered Cambridge to embark on his reasonably happy but undistinguished career at St John's College.

At university he soon realized that the thorough grounding he had received at Hawkshead in Euclid and algebra gave him a year's start over the other freshmen and he was able to spend much of his time 'reading nothing but classic authors according to my fancy, and Italian poetry'. He later regretted the amount

FACING PAGE: *Windermere Ferry, much used by William as a boy.*
(Carlisle City Library.)
    I bounded down the hill, shouting amain
    A lusty summons to the farther shore
    For the old Ferryman . . .

ABOVE: *Blea Tarn, between Great and Little Langdale.*
    . . . full many a spot
    Of hidden beauty have I chanced to espy
    Among the mountains; never one like this;
    So lonesome, and so perfectly secure . . .

of time he squandered on enjoying himself, but in these early days Cambridge provided a glittering contrast to his former life: 'the weeks went roundly on, with invitations, suppers, wine and fruit'.

He described his room over the noisy college kitchens as 'a nook obscure', relishing the fact that nearby was the statue of one of Cambridge's most illustrious former students, Isaac Newton, a man whose life and works William much admired.

Despite the crowded activities of university life he frequently had 'melancholy thoughts' about his future and soon found that the gregarious bustle of student activities left him unsatisfied. He would withdraw alone, to walk among the 'level fields' and meditate on life. Thus his first term passed 'pleasingly away', at times joining in the hectic social life, at others retreating into solitude. On one occasion he joined a party in the rooms formerly occupied by one of his greatest heroes, Milton, and became so intoxicated in drinking to the memory of the eminent poet that his 'brain reel'd . . . clouded by the fumes of wine' and he was nearly late for chapel.

The Master of St John's died soon after Wordsworth arrived and, as was the custom, the coffin was placed in the college hall where students left copies of their verses in homage to their former Master. Wordsworth however felt little inclination to do likewise and his uncle, Dr William Cookson, a Fellow of St John's, was astonished that his nephew should neglect this 'fair opportunity' for distinguishing himself.

William could not share his uncle's feelings and later wrote 'I did not, however, regret that I had been silent on this occasion, as I felt no interest in the deceased person, with whom I had no intercourse, and whom I had never seen but during his walks in the College grounds'. Thus Wordsworth's pride, already noted in his childhood was now a permanent part of his make-up and in years to come was to tax the patience of his closest friends and admirers. Many years after, Thomas de Quincey attributed his estrangement from Wordsworth to this: 'Never describe Wordsworth as equal in pride to Lucifer: no; but if you have occasion to write a life of Lucifer, set down that by possibility, in respect of pride, he might be some type of Wordsworth.'

His first summer vacation from Cambridge in 1788 was mostly spent in Hawkshead at Ann Tyson's. In his autobiographical poem *The Prelude* he records his rapture at seeing his native Lake District after nine months' absence, and he remembers his delight in

*

FACING PAGE, ABOVE: '*In the month of October 1787, I was sent to St John's College, Cambridge, of which my Uncle, Dr Cookson, had been a fellow.*'

FACING PAGE, BELOW LEFT: *William's small room above the kitchen overlooked Trinity College Chapel.*

FACING PAGE, BELOW RIGHT: *William aged 36, by Henry Edridge.*

RIGHT: *Elterwater. 'Within so narrow a compass, may be found an equal variety in the influences of light and shadow upon the sublime or beautiful features of landscape.'('Guide to the Lakes'.)*

seeing again familiar places and familiar things: Ann Tyson the kindly 'aged dame' who had become a second mother to him; her terrier dog; the 'snow white church' on the hill; and that particular delight all travellers experience on coming home:

> The joy with which I laid me down at night
> In my accustomed bed . . .

This holiday was an important phase in William's life. He had left Hawkshead the previous autumn an inexperienced though sensitive country boy; he returned a sophisticated and thoughtful young man, seeing his physical surroundings with a sharpened awareness, meditating deeply on the nature of life and viewing with new eyes the people around him. Some observations caused him pain, such as the now empty seat formerly used by an old man to sun himself; others were pleasant: the 'pale-fac'd babes' of nine months before, now 'rosy prattlers, tottering up and down'.

Returning to Cambridge in the autumn, the 'days of mirth and nights of revelry' faded in his memory and he settled down to a more solitary life, reading widely and finding more time for reflection.

In July 1790 William and his undergraduate friend, Robert Jones, left for a walking tour in France and Switzerland, returning to college in October. Christmas was spent with Dorothy at their uncle's rectory near Norwich and the following January William graduated and left Cambridge for a spell in London. Later he visited Robert Jones at his North Wales home and together they rambled through the Welsh hills. Their night-time ascent of Snowdon left a profound impression on William as he climbed above the mist to find the surrounding peaks suddenly illuminated by the moon,

Continued on page 12

ABOVE: *Snowdon from Llyn Nantle by Richard Wilson. William's night-time ascent of the mountain to see the sunrise left a powerful impression on his mind. He describes his mystical experience in* The Prelude, *the autobiographical poem, published posthumously.* (*The Walker Art Gallery, Liverpool.*)

FACING PAGE, ABOVE: *Thomas de Quincey (1785-1859), author of* Confessions of an English Opium Eater, *idolized Wordsworth, although they disagreed in later life. He rented Dove Cottage after Wordsworth moved, in 1809 and lived there until 1830.* (*National Portrait Gallery.*)

FACING PAGE, BELOW: *Rydal Waterfall, by Joseph Wright of Derby.* (*Derby Art Gallery.*)

Wordsworth properties open to the public

Wordsworth's birthplace, Cockermouth
    (National Trust)
Grammar School, Hawkshead
Dove Cottage and Museum, Grasmere
Rydal Mount, near Ambleside
Wordsworth Rooms, near Keswick

providing a 'universal spectacle . . . shaped for admiration and delight'.

Late in 1791 he decided to leave for France, spending a short period in Paris before moving to Orléans 'with a view to being out of the way of my own countrymen, that I might learn to speak the language fluently'.

This second visit to the Continent was much more eventful and significant. The revolutionary politics of France were contagious and he became a convert (albeit a temporary one) to the cause of republicanism. At Orléans he fell in love with Annette Vallon who gave birth to their daughter Caroline in December 1792. The details of this romance will probably remain forever shrouded in mystery. They clearly intended to marry but the combined effects of France's declaration of war and the Vallon family's hostility towards him probably account for their separation, and he returned to England, alone, before his daughter's birth.

Christmas was spent at Whitehaven and from April to December 1794 William and Dorothy stayed on and off at Windebrowe, a farmhouse which is just outside Keswick. The Calvert Trust have thoughtfully restored part of the ground floor of the house which is open to the public.

It was here that Dorothy began to act as her brother's secretary, copying down his poems and under his

ABOVE: 'The People taking the Tuileries', 20 June 1792.

LEFT: *Caroline Vallon, Wordsworth's illegitimate daughter by Annette Vallon whom he met at Orleans in 1792, during the French Revolution. William visited Annette prior to his marriage in 1802.*

supervision adding, deleting and modifying; a task she performed admirably for many years to come.

In May brother and sister visited their birthplace in Cockermouth, only to find it empty and (in Dorothy's words) '. . . in ruin, the terrace-walk buried and choked up with the old privet hedge which had formerly been so beautiful . . . the same hedge where the sparrows were used to build their nests'.

In January 1795 Wordsworth inherited £900, a much needed boost to his finances. In the autumn of 1795 a friend allowed them a rent-free house at Racedown, Dorset, their income being supplemented by £50 per year for looking after a child.

Had chance not led them to take up residence among these quiet hills the course of their lives might have been very different. For as a result of their settling in the west country they met Samuel Taylor Coleridge and his brother-in-law Robert Southey. In the years ahead the close relationship between William, Dorothy and Coleridge was a source of great joy and creativity for all three. William, Dorothy and their infant charge moved to Alfoxden in order to be closer to Coleridge's

ABOVE: *Bassenthwaite Lake 'ought to be circumnavigated'.*
  Spirit that knows no insulated spot,
  No chasm, no solitude; from link to link
  It circulates, the soul of all the worlds.

ABOVE RIGHT: *One of the Wordsworth Rooms at Windebrowe.*

RIGHT: *Wordsworth's visit to Castlerigg Circle in 1799 was marred by vandals who had whitewashed the prehistoric stones.*

Nether Stowey home. Alfoxden House was 'a large mansion, in a large park, with seventy head of deer'—a lovely setting for their friendship with Coleridge, a frequent visitor, to deepen.

All three embarked on a walking tour during which Coleridge began his famous ballad 'The Rime of the Ancient Mariner'. Wordsworth at first proffered help and advice but withdrew when he realized that their respective styles 'agreed so little'. He did however make several critical suggestions (which he later dismissed as 'trifling contributions'), including the idea of the shooting of the albatross.

Coleridge in turn encouraged William, urging him (largely without success) to embark on a long philosophical poem. 1797 and 1798 were fruitful years for William too, producing as he did 'The Ruined Cottage', 'Tintern Abbey', the 'Lucy' poems, and other works which were published in *Lyrical Ballads*.

After visiting Germany (where his great auto-biographical poem *The Prelude* was first conceived) William returned to England, spending a little time with the Hutchinsons at Sockburn before going on a walking tour of the Lake District with Coleridge towards the end of 1799.

Wordsworth was intent on showing Coleridge his 'native regions' and any walker today following their route could not have a better introduction to the glorious variety of Lakeland scenery. Beginning well to the east at Temple Sowerby they walked via Barton to Bampton (Haweswater) where they spent the night. Next day they ambled by the lakeside and climbed over into Longsleddale to Kentmere to spend their second night. Then over the Garburn Pass and along Windermere (crossing by the ferry) to Hawkshead.

Like most travellers returning after a long absence to the scenes of a happy childhood, Wordsworth was apprehensive:

> Remembrance of myself and of my peers
> Will press me down; to think of what is gone
> Will be an awful thought . . .

But in the event he was not unduly depressed, despite a number of changes in the preceding years. Not least of these was the death of Ann Tyson at the age of eighty-three. He remarks on that common phenomenon on returning to old haunts: 'So narrow seemed the brooks, the fields so small!' but found that 'the weight of sadness was in wonder lost'. After Hawkshead they spent five nights at Grasmere before making their way over Dunmail Raise via Bassenthwaite to Buttermere, thence to Wasdale Head and back to Keswick (via Borrowdale) where they parted company.

It was on this tour that William first saw Dove Cottage at Town End, Grasmere. He wrote to Dorothy:

Continued on page 19

★

ABOVE LEFT: *Samuel Taylor Coleridge (1772–1834) enjoyed a close friendship with the Wordsworths and their early admiration for each other was boundless. (National Portrait Gallery.)*

ABOVE: *Robert Southey (1774–1843), Coleridge's brother-in-law, was created Poet Laureate in 1813. He lived in Keswick from 1802 and is buried in Crosthwaite churchyard. (National Portrait Gallery.)*

FACING PAGE, ABOVE: *Weymouth Bay by John Constable. 'I think of Wordsworth, for on that spot perished his brother in the wreck of the "Abergavenny"'—Constable. (National Gallery.)*

FACING PAGE, BELOW: *'Lines composed a few miles above Tintern Abbey' is one of Wordsworth's most impressive poems. The painting is by Edward Dayes (Whitworth Art Gallery, Manchester.)*

ABOVE LEFT: *Wastwater and Great Gable, 'stern and desolate'.*
ABOVE RIGHT: *Keswick Lake (Derwent Water) by J. M. W. Turner.*
LEFT: *Sunset across Lake Windermere.*
FACING PAGE, BELOW: *Keswick Lake by Francis Towne. (Leeds City Art Gallery.)*

From his boyhood to his death, Wordsworth never lost his love of the Lake District. Indeed he did much of his composing out of doors. As he grew older he became increasingly concerned about the protection of his beloved Lakeland scenery. In his 'Guide', he actually foresaw the creation of the National Park when he wrote of the '. . . persons of pure taste throughout the whole island, who, by their visits (often repeated) to the lakes in the North of England, testify that they deem the district a sort of national property, in which every man has a right and interest who has an eye to perceive and a heart to enjoy'. His 'Sonnet on the Projected Kendal and Windermere Railway' composed in 1844 might still serve as a manifesto for conservationists:

>Is then no nook of English ground secure
>From rash assault? Schemes of retirement sown
>In youth, and 'mid the busy world kept pure
>As when their earliest flowers of hope were blown,
>Must perish;—how can they this blight endure?
>And must he too the ruthless change bemoan
>Who scorns a false utilitarian lure
>'Mid his paternal fields at random thrown?

16

18

'Coleridge was much struck with Grasmere and its neighbourhood . . . there is a small house at Grasmere empty, which, perhaps, we may take . . .'.

By late December 1799 William and Dorothy had moved into Dove Cottage in time to celebrate Dorothy's twenty-eighth birthday on Christmas Day. Here they remained for the next eight years, during which time some of the finest poetry in English was written.

In their time there Dove Cottage was unnamed— referred to simply as 'Town End'; it was formerly an inn, the Dove and Olive Branch, and it was only named Dove Cottage after the Wordsworths left.

Within a few months Coleridge came to live at Greta Hall, Keswick and there was much to-ing and fro-ing between the two houses. The distance from Keswick to Grasmere is thirteen miles and they had to climb over Dunmail Raise. But all three were strong walkers—Dorothy could cover the distance in four and a half hours, and Coleridge, for variation, might include an ascent of Helvellyn, one of England's highest hills!

Much of the scenery of the Lake District remains as it was in Wordsworth's time although Leatheswater, which all three frequently passed on their visits to each other, has been much enlarged to produce the Thirlmere reservoir. Fortunately we have John Constable's atmospheric painting of the lake to give us some idea of what it must have been like.

Fortunately, too, we have Dorothy's beautifully written journal, recording, often in great detail, life at Town End. Indeed she describes many incidents from which her brother produced some of his most memorable poetry and to read Dorothy's journal in conjunction with the verses written by William during the same period provides a unique insight into, and understanding of, their life together. William's poem about the daffodils is one of the most memorized poems in English; Dorothy's journal sheds fresh light on it and reveals that William was accompanied by her and not in fact wandering 'lonely as a cloud':

(Thursday April, 15th 1802.)
When we were in the woods beyond Gowbarrow Park we saw a few daffodils close to the water-side. We fancied that the lake had floated the seeds ashore, and that the little colony had so sprung up. But as we went along there were more and yet more; and at last, under the boughs of the trees, we saw that there was a long belt of them along the shore, about the breadth of a country turnpike road. I never saw daffodils so beautiful. They grew among the mossy stones about and about them; some rested their heads upon these stones as on a pillow for weariness; and the rest tossed and reeled and danced, and seemed as if they verily laughed with the wind . . . they looked so gay, ever glancing ever changing . . .

These years at Dove Cottage were ones of great happiness. The exquisite setting (in those days the house enjoyed an uninterrupted view across the lake) and in particular the small garden at the back ('our orchard') gave them tremendous pleasure. Dorothy tended their garden with loving care and meticulously records her work: 'Transplanted radishes after break-fast . . . sowed French beans and weeded . . . stuck peas, watered . . . and planted Brocoli . . . planted honeysuckle round the yew tree' and so on. Not that life was entirely idyllic. The journals also describe the illnesses and discomforts of their lives: 'Very sick and ill when I got home—went to bed in the sitting-room—took laudanum . . . a sore thumb from a cut . . . I was unwell and went to bed at eight o'clock . . . I was bad in my bowels' etc. Nor did William always enjoy the best of health: 'William had slept poorly . . . William went to bed very ill' are the kind of entries which recur. Dorothy's life was nothing if not varied. Bouts of ironing and washing would alternate with secretarial tasks, copying down her brother's greatest poetry. She devoured books, and records, among others, reading Chaucer, Smollett's life, Lessing's fables (which she translated) and the life of Ben Jonson.

Continued on page 22

*

FACING PAGE, ABOVE: *Grasmere Lake and Village from Red Bank. The Wordsworths enjoyed picnics on the small island.*

FACING PAGE, BELOW: *Dove Cottage and garden.*
Where once the Dove and Olive-Bough
Offered a greeting of good ale
To all who entered Grasmere Vale;
And called on him who must depart
To leave it with a jovial heart;
There, where the Dove and Olive-Bough
Once hung, a Poet harbours now,
A simple water-drinking Bard . . .

RIGHT: *Wordsworth in 1818 by B. R. Haydon. (National Portrait Gallery.)*

TOP: *Dove Cottage by Wordsworth's daughter, Dora. The road shown was the main Kendal-Keswick route, which, until the present main road was built in 1831, ran by the cottage. The yew tree on the right can still be seen.*

LEFT: *The upstairs bedroom used first by William, and later by Dorothy. The bed is from Rydal Mount.*

ABOVE: *Inkstand belonging to Wordsworth. (Dove Cottage.)*

FACING PAGE, ABOVE: *Page from Dorothy's journal, 15 April 1802. The famous daffodils at Gowbarrow are described.*

FACING PAGE, ABOVE RIGHT: *Dorothy Wordsworth and 'little Miss Belle', a late portrait (1833) by S. Crosthwaite which hangs in the library at Rydal Mount.*

FACING PAGE, RIGHT: *Upstairs sitting room at Dove Cottage.*

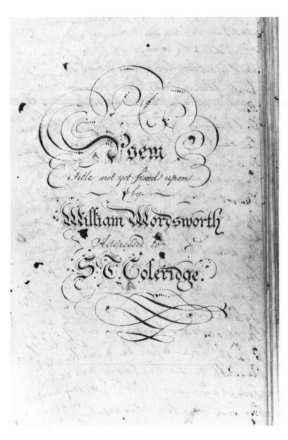

She seems constantly to have been either writing to Coleridge or eagerly anticipating a letter from him. And if the number of times she records baking pies is any guide, they all enjoyed prodigious appetites.

By the summer of 1800 the first edition of *Lyrical Ballads* had sold out and a two-volume second edition was prepared and published in January 1801. The anonymity of the first edition was abandoned to the extent that Wordsworth's name—but not Coleridge's—now appeared on the title page. The poems of Coleridge from the first edition were repeated in the second; William contributed several additional works, including 'Michael' and 'Hart-Leap Well', and he also added an important Preface, setting out in detail his aims in publishing poems 'so materially different from those upon which general approbation is at present bestowed'.

Here Wordsworth made his famous statement: 'Poetry is the spontaneous overflow of powerful feelings: it takes its origin from emotion recollected in tranquillity.' He revealed that his main aim was 'to make the incidents of common life interesting by tracing in them . . . the primary laws of our nature'.

This deep concern to extract universal truths from 'the incidents of common life' was accompanied by a strong desire to find a suitable form of language in which to express his feelings and ideas appropriately. He eschewed elaborate imagery and embraced a simpler, direct style which at the same time could be pure and elevated. Indeed the simplicity of the language in, for instance, the 'Lucy' poems actually adds to the powerful emotions:

> She lived unknown, and few could know
> When Lucy ceased to be;
> But she is in her grave, and, oh,
> The difference to me!

And there can be few more elemental descriptions of the finality of death than the short verse:

> No motion has she now, no force;
> She neither hears nor sees;
> Rolled round in earth's diurnal course,
> With rocks, and stones, and trees.

Much of William's poetry was composed out of doors, usually whilst walking up and down and speaking out loud. Composition certainly did not always come effortlessly and Dorothy often records that her brother worked long and hard: 'Wm could not compose much, fatigued himself with altering . . . William worked all the morning . . . but in vain . . . William worked at The Ruined Cottage and made himself very ill.' His 'fight for words' would frequently leave him exhausted.

*

TOP LEFT: The Prelude (MS B), title page: 'Poem/Title not yet fixed upon/by/William Wordsworth/Addressed to/S. T. Coleridge'.

LEFT: The Prelude (MS B), 'Book First/Introduction, Childhood & School time'. The title was provided posthumously by Mary.

FACING PAGE: Sir Walter Scott by Sir Henry Raeburn. The painting can be seen at Abbotsford, Scott's home. William and Dora visited Scott in 1831, their final meeting.

Even so, these early years of the century were productive ones, during which time he laboured hard on some of his major works—not least the story of the leech gatherer in 'Resolution and Independence', and one of his most memorable short poems belongs to this same period:

My heart leaps up when I behold
　A rainbow in the sky:
So was it when my life began;
So is it now I am a man;
So be it when I shall grow old,
　Or let me die!
The Child is father of the Man;
And I could wish my days to be
Bound each to each by natural piety.

His greatest poem of all 'Ode: Intimations of Immortality from Recollections of Early Childhood' with its magnificently arresting and poignant opening, also dates from this time:

There was a time when meadow, grove, and stream,
The earth, and every common sight,
　To me did seem
　Apparelled in celestial light,
The glory and the freshness of a dream.
It is not now as it hath been of yore;—
　Turn whereso'er I may,
　　By night or day,
The things which I have seen I now can see no more.

In the summer of 1802 the Wordsworths' financial fortunes experienced a dramatic improvement: the long-standing debt owed to them by Lord Lonsdale (their father's employer) was largely settled, making William and Dorothy comparatively well off. They left for the Continent to visit Annette and Caroline. We know little of the details of their time together in France and when they returned to England, William married Mary Hutchinson, his childhood companion. Returning to Dove Cottage in October 1802 with his bride and sister, William now had two devoted females to look after him.

Dorothy seems over the years to have coped well with the fact of William's marriage and with the difficulties of them all living in such close proximity. No one can doubt the passionate devotion which Dorothy had for her brother; the wedding day was an unbearable ordeal for her, and she lay prostrate and helpless on her bed for much of the morning, quite overcome by the thought of William's marriage. Mary later recorded that they did not receive a single wedding present, due largely one suspects to the lukewarm attitude towards the match by some of Mary's relations.

They remained at Dove Cottage until 1808, enjoying on the whole a happy and contented life, receiving many visitors and guests but travelling away only very occasionally. Coleridge's increasing ill health was a source of great anxiety and the death of William's brother John—drowned in a shipwreck off Portland Bill—caused them considerable grief. But there were more happy times too: the tour of Scotland which included a visit to Sir Walter Scott, and which inspired a number of poems, was a highlight of this period, which creatively was dominated by a major poetic achievement; the completion in 1805 of an early version of *The Prelude*.

In 1807 Wordsworth published *Poems in Two Volumes* containing most of his work (with the exception of *The Prelude*) written since the publication of the second edition of *Lyrical Ballads*. The collection of 1807 enjoyed a very mixed reception, difficult to appreciate today when many of the poems have become established favourites: 'Resolution and Independence', 'My heart leaps up', 'I wandered lonely as a cloud', the 'Intimations Ode', 'The Solitary Reaper' and such sonnets as 'Composed upon Westminster Bridge'. The witty review writers of the time had a field-day, ridiculing Wordsworth's interests in aspects of the world they considered trivial and beneath the notice of serious writers. It was not for the first time in literary history that a great artist had to suffer the indignity of seeing his work mutilated and misunderstood by blinkered critics unwilling to consider new approaches which diverged from the accepted tastes and conventions of the age. The youthful Byron called the poems 'trash' and dismissed them as 'namby pamby'. Robert Southey admired the political sonnets as 'truly philosophical and heroic' but was unsympathetic towards many of the 'simpler' poems. He accused Wordsworth of looking at 'pile-worts and daffodowndillies through the same telescope which he applies to the moon and stars', and castigated him for finding 'subjects for philosophizing and fine feeling in every peasant and vagabond . . .'. Wordsworth's radical and revolutionary way of revealing

24

truth in life and nature would have to wait some time before enjoying a wide and popular acceptance. He partly feigned indifference to the misunderstandings, the ridicule and the disdain, but to one so proud, rather humourless, and absolutely certain of his worth, it must have been deeply galling. Not that he took the criticism in complete silence. He could respond to the 'London Wits and Witlings' with zest, accusing them of insensitivity and shallowness. Writing to Lady Beaumont he expresses with great dignity his firm conviction that his work would long outlive the jibes of clever reviewers:

> Trouble not yourself upon the present reception of these poems; of what moment is that compared with what I trust is their destiny, to console the afflicted, to add sunshine to daylight by making the happy happier, to teach the young and the gracious of every age to see, to think and feel, and therefore to become more actively and securely virtuous; this is their office, which I trust they will faithfully perform long after we (that is, all that is mortal of us) are mouldered in our graves.

Time has proved him right and these verses truly did profoundly affect the attitudes of future ages. But to an older generation of readers whose tastes had been formed in the age of Johnson, with a commitment to the advances of a scientific enlightenment, the early Romantics seemed, as we would say today, to be on quite a different wavelength. A new age had dawned in which writers and painters were seeing 'into the heart of things'. Blake could perceive ' . . . a world in a Grain of Sand, and a Heaven in a wild flower' just as Wordsworth could find that ' . . . the meanest flower that blows can give/Thoughts that do often lie too deep for tears'.

It would be wrong to imagine the Romantic poets spending their entire time producing such sublime and elevated writing. Like most of their contemporaries in other walks of life they had to grapple with the harsh realities of 19th-century existence. And Wordsworth was no exception. The high child mortality rate of that time is a known historical fact, but to the Wordsworth family it was a fact of daily life. They felt deeply for their fellows who suffered death and hardship and poverty. Nor were they themselves entirely immune; two of their own children died very young.

By the time they moved to Allan Bank in 1808, Mary had given birth to two sons (John and Thomas)

*

FACING PAGE, ABOVE: *Leathes Water (Thirlmere) by John Constable, 1806. Wordsworth and Constable greatly admired each other's work. (Tate Gallery.)*

FACING PAGE, LEFT: *Lowther Castle, home of William Lowther, the first Earl of Lonsdale (second creation). Wordsworth energetically supported the Tory Lowthers in the 1818 Westmorland election.*

ABOVE RIGHT: *'View from Rydal Park' by Francis Towne. (Leeds City Art Gallery.)*

RIGHT: *The porch at Rydal Mount, William's final home from 1813 to 1850. In 1812 two of the Wordsworth children died and were buried in Grasmere. The move to Rydal enabled the grief-stricken family to avoid these unhappy Grasmere associations.*

and a daughter (Dora). A second daughter (Catherine) and a son (William, their last child) were born during their two years at Allan Bank. In 1811 they moved to Grasmere parsonage and it was here, a year later, that Catherine and Thomas died.

The family's final move was in 1813 when they settled in the beautifully positioned Rydal Mount which, like Dove Cottage, is now open to the public. It would be foolish to dismiss the remaining thirty-seven years of William's life as being unworthy of our attention, though some commentators have sought to do so. These later years were by no means barren of achievement, but his successes were of a different order and he rarely produced work to match the poems found in *Lyrical Ballads* and *Poems in Two Volumes*.

His life at Rydal was made the more comfortable as a result of his appointment to the office of Distributor of Stamps, which carried with it a salary of £300. As he became better off his views about society changed, though whether this is a case of cause and effect is difficult to ascertain. Certainly he was no longer the radical and revolutionary thinker of his youth. He espoused now the values of an Anglican Tory and by 1832 actually opposed the Reform Bill, though he always championed the anti-slavery cause. And whilst he was vociferous about the inhumanity of factory work, he also harangued the railways for 'transferring at once large bodies of uneducated persons' to the Lake District.

Many reasons have been put forward to account for Wordsworth's marked change, and his increasingly opinionated and egotistical manner: the drying up of his poetic genius; his estrangement from Coleridge who under the influence of opium had become a figure of pity; the fear of the effects of popular poitical unrest; these are just some of the suggested causes. Not that his late life was entirely bereft of success. In 1820 the publication in one volume of the Duddon Sonnet Sequence, with his prose *Guide through the District of the Lakes*, was well received. Soon the guide went into a separate edition and became an established favourite. By 1835 a fifth edition 'with considerable additions' was printed and it remains one of the best introductions for visitors to the region. Also in 1835 William's poetic genius enjoyed a sudden late-flowering in 'Extempore Effusion upon the Death of James Hogg', an elegiac poem which ranks among the best in our language.

It was gratifying to Wordsworth to achieve increasing

Continued on page 32

★

FACING PAGE, ABOVE: *Rydal Mount's 4½ acres were landscaped and terraced by William. He advocated informal gardens which harmonized with the surrounding countryside. His summer house can also be seen. Rydal Mount is owned by a descendant of William.*

FACING PAGE, BELOW LEFT: *The library at Rydal Mount, 1840.*

FACING PAGE, BELOW RIGHT: *Dora Wordsworth (1804-1847) William's favourite child. She married Edward Quillinan in 1841.*

ABOVE RIGHT: *Mary Wordsworth, William's kindly and devoted wife. De Quincey noted her 'considerable obliquity of vision'.*

RIGHT: *William was highly pleased when his Cambridge College (St John's) commissioned this portrait in 1832.*

FACING PAGE, ABOVE: *Birks Bridge, and the River Duddon.*

. . . Duddon! as I cast my eyes,
I see what was, and is, and will abide;
Still glides the Stream, and shall forever glide;
The Form remains, the Function never dies.

FACING PAGE, BELOW LEFT: *Wordsworth's Stamp Office, Ambleside, by John Harden, 1834. (Abbot Hall Art Gallery.)*

FACING PAGE, BELOW RIGHT: *'Miss Wordsworth' 1842, by John Harden (1772-1847) of Brathay Hall. He was a gifted amateur artist. (Abbot Hall Art Gallery.)*

ABOVE: *Wordsworth's grandchildren. William's eldest son, John, married Isabella Curwen in 1830. This charming portrait is in Belle Isle, the round house on the largest of Windermere's islands. The house and island are open to the public during the summer.*

FACING PAGE, ABOVE: *Costume Ball at Buckingham Palace 6 June 1845, where William was presented to Queen Victoria. His other encounter with royalty took place five years previously at Rydal Mount, when he received the Dowager Queen Adelaide. (Reproduced by gracious permission of Her Majesty Queen Elizabeth II. The Royal Library, Windsor Castle.)*

FACING PAGE, LEFT: *Dora's Field, Rydal, bought by William for £300 with the intention of building a house there. (National Trust.)*

ABOVE: *Haydon's portrait (1842) of William against a background depicting Helvellyn, which Wordsworth last climbed at the age of seventy. It was Haydon who, many years before, introduced Wordsworth to the young poet, John Keats. This painting inspired Elizabeth Barrett Browning's sonnet 'Wordsworth on Helvellyn'. (National Portrait Gallery.)*

fame and recognition as he grew older. On his visits to London he was much in demand by fashionable society, and pilgrims were eager to pay homage at Rydal.

In 1842 Sir Robert Peel awarded him a Civil List Pension of £300 per year. The following year Robert Southey, who had been created Poet Laureate in 1813, died at Keswick and Wordsworth was now offered the position. At the age of 73 William felt he was too old to accept, but Peel persuaded him to change his mind. He even attended the Queen's Ball and his friends of earlier days would have found it ironic to contemplate the great exponent of 'plain living and high thinking' in court dress and cocked hat.

To live to a great age is never an unmixed blessing and it was inevitable that William should frequently suffer the grief of losing friends and loved ones. In particular the death of his daughter Dora in 1847 left him distraught. In addition Dorothy's mental decline during her later life was a source of much anguish, although she outlived him by five years.

In the spring of 1850 William caught a cold on a country walk; pleurisy set in and he died on St George's Day, eighty years to the month after his birth. His wife survived him by nine years and they share the simplest of gravestones in Grasmere churchyard, now one of the most visited literary shrines in the world.

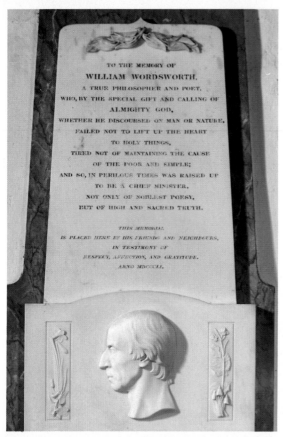

> Our birth is but a sleep and a forgetting:
> The Soul that rises with us, our life's Star,
>   Hath had elsewhere its setting,
>   And cometh from afar:
>   Not in entire forgetfulness,
>   And not in utter nakedness,
> But trailing clouds of glory do we come
>   From God, who is our home.

(From 'Intimations of Immortality'.)

TOP: *Grasmere Church and* (BELOW) *William and Mary's grave. Other members of the family are buried close by.*

LEFT CENTRE: *Wordsworth's memorial inside Grasmere Church. The inscription was composed by the Oxford theologian, John Keble.*

BACK COVER: *Gowbarrow Park, Ullswater, where Dorothy and William together came across the 'host of golden daffodils'.*

ACKNOWLEDGMENTS

The author received invaluable help from Dr Peter Laver, Resident Librarian at the Wordsworth Library, Dove Cottage. He is also grateful to Mr and Mrs D. Crosbie, Wordsworth's Birthplace; Mrs Mary Henderson (née Wordsworth) and her curators Mr and Mrs D. Brookes, Rydal Mount; Mr and Mrs George Kirkby, Dove Cottage; J. A. Nettleton, MBE, Lake District National Park Centre, Brockhole. Thanks are also due to Mr E. A. Bowness, Neil Hall, Mrs Mollie Hargreaves, Mrs E. J. Hartley and Dr W. Rollinson.

PICTURES: pp i Dept. of Rare Books, Cornell University Library, U.S.A.; ii, 1, 3, (below R), 8 (below R), 20 (above), 21 (above L), 22, 26 (below L & R), 27 (above) by kind permission of the Trustees of Dove Cottage; 1 (autograph), 24 (below) Mary Evans Picture Library; iv, 2 C. Hanson-Smith, National Trust; 3 (above), 18 (below R), 20 (below L & R), 21 (below), 32 (below) Bob Matthews; 3 (below L), 5, 30 (below) A. F. Kersting, AIIP, FRPS; 4, 7, 9, 13 (above & below), 16, 18 (above & below L), 25 (below), 28 (above), 32 (above) E. A. Bowness; 6 Carlisle City Library; 8 (above) Sydney W. Newbery, Hon FIIP, FRPS; 8 (below L), 27 (below) the Master and Fellows of St John's College, Cambridge; 10 The Walker Art Gallery, Liverpool; 11 (above), 14, 19, 31 National Portrait Gallery, by kind permission of the Trustees; 11 (below), 28 (below L & R) Abbot Hall Art Gallery, Kendal (A. S. Clay Collection); 12 (above) The Mansell Collection; 12 (below) Mme Blanchet (Weidenfeld & Nicolson Archives); 13 (centre) The Calvert Trust; 15 (above) The National Gallery, London, by courtesy of the Trustees; 15 (below) The Whitworth Art Gallery, University of Manchester; 17 (above) Fotomas Index; 17 (below), 25 (above) Leeds City Art Gallery; 21 (above R), 26 (above) by kind permission of Mrs Mary Henderson, Rydal Mount; 23 by kind permission of Mrs Maxwell-Scott, OBE; 24 (above) John Webb, Tate Gallery, by courtesy of the Trustees; 29 by kind permission of Mr E. S. C. Curwen, Belle Isle; 30 (above) The Royal Library, Windsor Castle; 32 (centre) Geoffrey Blake, Woodmansterne Ltd.

ISBN 0 85372 324 9